Journey

into the

Spirit Realm

Journey into the Spirit Realm

A Practical Guide to Unlocking Seer Encounters

RITA LO

Editing by Sarah Wind

ISBN 9798648748231

First Edition: June 2020

This book is dedicated
To God who's my comforter and teacher
and
To Rick for being my friend and encourager

CONTENTS

INTRODUCTION

Thank you from the bottom of my heart for purchasing this book. It was on my heart to write for a number of years, but this book only came to fruition after a dream I had in January 2020. In the dream, I was at my house (which I own) and there were guests that wanted to check out all the rooms. They insisted that they hadn't seen all the rooms yet, which puzzled me because I knew that I had shown them the whole house. "What other rooms could there be in my small house?" I thought to myself.

I went to investigate what my guests were talking about and to my surprise, they were right! There were in fact three rooms in the house that I was completely unaware of. Then I suddenly remembered that the three rooms had always been there. My guests were very excited about the discovery and couldn't wait to see the new rooms. To my dismay, the rooms were in complete disarray, so I told them they could not see the rooms. I felt guilty for saying, "No," to my guests and then I woke up.

This was the second or third time I had a dream about hidden rooms in my house. I knew that God wanted to tell me something and that it must be important. I am not very skilled at dream interpretation, so I immediately started asking God what the dream meant. I had to keep asking God until He answered my question.

He told me that the house represented my whole self, and the rooms represented parts of my being. I knew what God was saying to me. It was time for me to share every part of myself with the world, even the messy parts. I had felt for a long time that God wanted me to share and not hide, because sharing has the potential to bless a lot of people.

There are parts of myself that I don't normally share, and when people find out about them, they are either really excited to know more (like in the dream) or they become jealous. These parts include my daily encounters in the spiritual realm and how I navigate life while seeing in the spirit. There are many reasons why I don't share, but basically, it comes down to two reasons. I don't like drawing attention to myself and I don't want to be boastful. I felt like the dream was a slap in the face saying, "Get over yourself. You need to share."

In the dream, I didn't even remember the three rooms were there until my guests started asking to see them. To me this said that I was so used to hiding certain parts of myself that I didn't even remember hiding anything. Hiding didn't work in my dream and it doesn't work in my real life either. What if I got over myself and showed my guests the hidden rooms? Would they have been blessed? I realized from this dream that I was doing a huge disservice to people by not sharing the gifts that God has given me.

I have written this book as a resource to help equip and encourage you in your seeing gift. I believe that every Christian can have the ability to see in the spirit realm. As it states in 1 Corinthians 14:1, "eagerly desire gifts of the Spirit," I encourage you to eagerly desire the gift of seeing (NIV). Seeing in the spirit realm every day has dramatically changed my life for the better, and I believe that it will change your life as well. I wasn't born with the gift of seeing. I only started seeing when I was 38 years old, so I know that you too can receive the gift of seeing at any point in your life.

In this book I will be sharing my testimony of coming to know the Father, Son, and Holy Spirit and my journey to seeing in the spirit realm. I won't be sharing a lot of Scripture or theology, but I will be sharing my personal experiences. Many things I've learned have happened by trying different things until something worked. My hope is to pass these keys on to you so that you don't have to learn things the hard way. At the same time, there isn't a guarantee that the way I see will be the exact same way you see. God is infinite and He can speak to you in whatever way He pleases. Think of this book as a springboard into diving into your own unique journey of seeing with the Lord. Everything that God had done for me, I pray that He will do it again in your life and more so!

My Journey Into Seeing Every Day

The journey of how I began seeing in the spiritual realm every day has not been an easy road. I didn't grow up in a Christian home, and I remember being very sad as a child. I thought my life was cursed the moment I was born. You see I'm a twin, but the doctors didn't know that my mother was going to have twins until the day of delivery. It was a complicated birth from what I was told. I had been crushing my brother in the womb, so he was placed in an incubator for a few days and received medical attention. I, on the other hand, seemed fine to the doctors, so no extra care was given to me. I always wondered if the doctors had spent just a little more time with me, would I have had irritable bowel syndrome (IBS), dyslexia, and a heart murmur? My brother had none of these problems.

Jumping forward to my 34th birthday, I had everything I ever wanted materially. I worked for a great company that paid really well and I owned a condo. Despite my success, I was very depressed. My marriage had failed for two main reasons: I couldn't have any children (because my IBS had gotten so bad due to the stress of the relationship) and I wasn't Christian. My ex-partner knew I wasn't Christian when we first met, and he assured me that it was completely okay with him. A couple of years later, it was no longer okay with him. He continually pressured me to become Christian and threatened me saying, "You're going to go to hell!" The argument that I would go to hell had no effect on me whatsoever. I didn't care what would happen to me after I died since my life up to that point had been hellish. I thought I was cursed, so I figured I was destined to go to hell anyway.

While we were in the process of breaking up, our mutual friends didn't want to pick sides, so they decided not to talk to either of us. It was very awkward since we all went to the same church. I only went to church to support my ex-partner, and I was not a Christian, even though I went with him for a couple of years.

There I was approaching my 34th birthday, which I considered the golden age for me to be married with children and finally be happy for the first time in my life. None of these things had happened, and on top of that my friends had disappeared. I cried every single day whenever I was alone for at least a month.

One night I had a dream. I was sitting in a completely

restored early 1960s Cadillac car with white leather seats. Then out of nowhere a single bullet flew straight at me and went through my chest. I knew instantly that I was dying, but I felt strangely peaceful with no fear. The next thing I knew, I saw endless bright lights all around me and a silhouette of a man wearing a robe coming toward me with open arms. I couldn't make out his face since it was densely covered with fog. He said to me in a commanding voice, "I forgive you of all your sins." I felt an internal warmth that I had never felt before, and was uncharacteristically happy, perhaps for the first time in my whole life. Just as the man was only a couple of inches away, ready to embrace me, I woke up.

I had no doubt in my mind that I had met God because my dream reminded me of movie scenes that portrayed God in Heaven. I was elated when I woke up. I had met God and He told me He forgave all my sins. I assumed that meant I was going to Heaven and that my ex-partner was completely wrong in saying that I was going to hell. I didn't think I needed to do anything else because I had assurance I was going to Heaven, so I didn't take any other steps to pray and make Jesus my Lord and Savior. The perpetual crying spell ended, but I was still far from being happy with my life.

A couple of months later, a friend from my past reached out and told me that she was going to look for a new church and she invited me to go with her. As soon I set foot in Livingwater Church, I immediately had a good impression. I was really curious because of what I was feeling, so I attended another service by myself. As worship music was playing and I was staring at the wall bored out of my mind, I heard a quiet voice, which I knew was God, say, "Go to church." I responded in my mind by saying, "Fine, but only for one year."

I agreed because I didn't want to disobey the All Mighty God who could kill me instantly, and I also wanted a safe place to meet new friends. There was another sinister reason too. I wanted to prove that Christians were idiots and wrong in their belief that Christianity was so great. I didn't understand how people could call themselves Christians and still hurt others deeply. Weren't they supposed to practice what they preached, like, "love thy neighbor"? Christians were the ones who had hurt me the most in my life. I believed in God, but I also believed in other spirits like Buddha, who answered some questions about my future when I went to a temple. I didn't understand why Christianity was considered the number one religion. Shouldn't we accept all cultures and not say one religion is better than another?

When my year attending church was up, I couldn't leave. A Bible study small group was happening at my condo every week, and I tried multiple times to convince the group to meet at a different location to no avail. It was odd to me that I was hosting a small group even though I wasn't a Christian, but they needed a place to meet. In addition, I took in a housemate who needed a place to stay who was an active church member, and she kept pressuring me to stay. I was so frustrated because I couldn't get anyone from Livingwater Church to leave! I knew this was all God's clever way to get me to keep attending, and I wasn't happy about it.

There was another reason why I wanted everyone to leave. I was going through a period of severe depression, and I didn't want to be around people. I didn't understand why I was feeling so down. My life was fairly good. I had made a ton of new friends, my job was still solid, and I had accepted the fact that I would be single forever with no children of my own. There was no good reason why I kept seeing images of hurting myself in different ways. I, of course, didn't tell anyone what was going on inside of me. I didn't want people to think I was crazy.

A church retreat was coming up and I wasn't planning to go because I had gotten really sick from the last retreat I attended. Two days before the retreat, I suddenly wanted to go. I knew it was last minute, but I decided to test if I was really meant to go by reaching out to the head pastor. I told him I wanted to go to the retreat, but if I couldn't get a ride back home one day early on Saturday night instead of Sunday (because of my job's schedule) I wasn't going to go at all. It took him nearly the whole day to get back to me, and I was hoping he wouldn't. To my surprise, he said he found a ride for me. I was touched that someone actually volunteered to drive me home a day early and miss part of the retreat.

While at the retreat, I kept thinking, "Why am I here since I am not even Christian?" I was the only non-Christian there. It was a small church of only about 100 people. In the morning session the guest speaker, Pastor Gab, said, "I don't normally do this, but I need everyone in the room to close your eyes now. Even the leaders, please close your eyes." He waited to make sure everyone's eyes were closed and then said, "Would the person who slit their wrists please stand up?" I was thinking, "That's not me. He must be talking about my guy friend who is depressed." I had never slit my wrists before, but I had definitely thought about it numerous times.

When no one stood up, he asked everyone to keep their eyes closed and then said, "There is a young lady who slit her wrists." At that point, I knew Pastor Gab was talking about me, but no way was I going to stand up. I didn't want anyone to know that I thought about hurting myself. When no one stood up again, Pastor Gab said, "I am not going to let anyone open their eyes until this person stands up, or at least puts a hand up." I finally relented and raised my hand because I didn't want to make people wait in silence any longer. Pastor Gab said a general prayer over me, and then finally allowed people to open their eyes. I thought that was the end of that.

To my disappointment, he didn't resume his sermon. He started to give out prophetic words instead. He said, "Anyone who has prophetic gifts, please stand up so I can pray over you." I knew I had a prophetic gift, but I was not going to stand up after what just happened. He then said, "There are four people in the room who are gifted," but only two stood up. I knew I was one, and I knew that my guy friend who was depressed was the other one.

Then Pastor Gab called out people who had issues with their father to stand up, and after that he called out people who had issues from their past to stand up. I didn't want to stand up for anything even though everything that he had called out applied to me. I finally stood up for the third thing he called out, because at that point he had started calling out specific people one by one in their seats.

When I stood up, a group of people came around me. It was the first time that I had so many people laying hands on me and praying over me at one time. With my eyes closed and my head bowed (because that was the Christian way to receive prayer), I could sense that Pastor Gab was in front of me. He touched my head with one hand and said, "You hate yourself." I immediately started bawling because that was very true.

The next thing I knew I woke up from a trance-like state as my friend tapped me on my shoulder and started praying for me. I was standing up with my eyes still closed and my head still bowed, which completely baffled me. I felt someone's hand on my head while my friend prayed for me, and the feeling only left after my friend finished praying.

Later I asked my friend to tell me what happened when he prayed for me because my eyes had been closed. He told me that I was standing, praying to myself, with no one around me. He really wanted to pray for me, so that's why he came over and tapped me on my shoulder. I asked him if Pastor Gab was next to him with his hand on my head and he said that no one else was praying for me. We looked at each other and concluded that it was either God or an angel touching me.

After the session everyone left the room and I got a chance to talk to Pastor Gab privately. I wanted to make sure he would not tell anyone that I had suicidal thoughts. He started prophesying over me about my relationship with God and I told him that I was not a Christian, even though God had spoken to me a couple of times. Pastor Gab looked at me with a bewildered expression. He assured me that he wasn't going to tell anyone that it was me who raised my hand, and he prayed for me once more. After talking to Pastor Gab, I felt a change within me that I couldn't explain.

Later on that night, a different friend drove me home and we got home at 2:00am. I didn't feel sick at all, which was completely shocking to me. My body would normally break down and be in pain when I didn't get enough sleep. I only felt tired. When I woke up the next morning, I had a smile on my face and my inside was smiling too. I felt like I had a plastered grin on my face like Joker from Batman. I had never in my whole life felt so joyful and so pain free. The chronic pain that I had been suffering from, because of my health and emotional issues, was completely gone. The difference was like night and day.

My car was still at church, so my housemate took me to go pick it up on Sunday morning. During our trip there, I wanted so badly to shake her to make her snap out of her dreary mood. When I arrived at church, everything had a slight glow. I realized that not only was I completely joyful, but my whole thought process had completely flipped. I saw everything in a positive light and I was feeling God's incredible love over me. I felt like I was in Heaven.

God spoke to me very clearly that morning saying, "You are not a mistake and I love you very much." I also felt Him call me into full-time ministry, which I didn't understand at the time. How would it be possible for me to do that? I couldn't just drop my whole career, which I had spent building for over a decade, to do what God wanted me to do. For me to go into ministry, I would need God's divine intervention. I didn't tell anyone at my church what God said to me that day.

It might seem like at that point I became a follower of Christ, but I would have said, "No," had anyone asked if I was a Christian. I still didn't want to be associated with Christians because they were the ones who had hurt me the most, and I couldn't easily forget that.

Two weeks went by and I was still feeling God's presence heavily on me. I believed I could do absolutely no wrong in

God's eyes, and I felt so accepted and loved by Him. Never had I ever felt so much love aimed directly toward me. During this time, almost everyone at my church said that I had changed dramatically. They would say things like I was glowing, or I seemed happier, or the load that I was carrying got lifted.

Only after realizing that I couldn't stop praising and thinking about God did I become aware that I was now a follower of Christ. "Crap," was the first word that came to mind after this realization. I was now associated with a group of people who I always tried my hardest to never become like.

One day I was stricken with a major panic attack and after that I didn't feel the presence of God anymore. It felt like something really great inside of me was violently ripped away and now I was an empty shell. I didn't feel like a complete and whole person anymore. I desperately wanted to feel God's presence again, but I didn't know who to turn to for help. My church wasn't a Pentecostal or Charismatic church and I didn't recall anyone there ever speaking about God's presence. I couldn't ask Pastor Gab for help since he had only been a guest speaker and he lived in Southern California. So, it was up to me to figure out the way back into God's presence.

I thought perhaps serving would get me back into God's presence again, but unfortunately it didn't. I received an idea from God to have the church's first ever toy drive during Christmas time, which was a success. After that, I was asked to co-lead other outreach events as well.

I also tried reading about the Holy Spirit and I started reading the Bible more with no luck. After a couple of months of trying different things, I still couldn't get into God's presence. I was getting burned out from serving in addition to working full time. One night I had a nightmare, which at first I dismissed thinking it was just an attack from the enemy, but then I had two more nightmares the following two nights. After the third sleepless night, I decided I was done with church and I wasn't going to serve or continue attending.

One thing I thought might be a key to re-entering God's presence was the gift of tongues. The first time I ever heard someone speak in tongues, I felt strangely comforted. I always felt in my spirit that I was going to receive a heavenly prayer language, but I resisted for at least a year. I didn't like the thought of losing control of my speech, because I had trust issues with God.

During an ordeal when I found out a blood relative had used my social security number to open a phone account, I was suffering from major anxiety attacks. I would get up and get ready in the morning, and then I had to lie down again because I was so mentally exhausted. After the third day of this, I heard God tell me that these attacks would stop immediately if I received my prayer language. I went to ask my housemate, who had the gift of tongues, to pray for me to receive the gift also. She wasn't sure if it would work since we weren't in a church setting, but I asked her to try anyway to see what would happen. She told me to say "hallelujah" over and over again while she spoke in tongues and was laying hands on me. Within five minutes, I received my heavenly language, and I knew that the attacks were over. Little did I know how much this gift would impact my life.

I decided to start speaking in tongues every day for at least 30 minutes to see if I could get closer to feeling God's presence again. Nothing happened after doing this for three months. I didn't feel anything at all when I prayed. I became very frustrated, but I wasn't going to quit, so I decided to try something else. My new plan to get God's attention was to scream at the top of my lungs in tongues while being completely focused on asking for more of God's presence. This exercise only lasted 20 minutes since my throat would start to hurt from all the screaming. I didn't feel God's presence, but I did feel heat throughout my whole body, which I thought was a great start.

I continued to pray this way almost every day until I started school at Bethel School of Supernatural Ministry (BSSM) in Redding, which is another key event I will share about in the next chapter. For the first couple of months, besides feeling heat consistently, sometimes I felt joy or the peace of God. Eventually I did feel God's presence every time I prayed this way.

After leaving Livingwater Church and not attending any church for about six months, my life became fairly peaceful and my nightmares were mostly gone. I had no intention of ever going back to church, which I didn't tell anyone. One day, my roommate and I visited a mutual friend at his new workplace. All three of us were conversing about my friend's new job when suddenly I felt God's presence in the room. I didn't want to say anything at first because I was trying to figure out what was going on. After a few minutes, my friend paused and then looked at me and said, "Why is God here?" I was shocked that he too could feel God's presence. The conversation quickly changed to be all about me. They talked about why I should go back to church, which churches I could go to that understood spiritual attacks, and an upcoming conference.

I felt God highlight the conference to me, so I went without knowing who the speaker was. My roommate happened to be the event organizer, so she was able to arrange for me to have a one-on-one prayer session with the speaker. The speaker blew me away with his prophetic words. He asked me if I was getting attacked at night and then he prayed over me and said he saw the afflicting spirits go away. I haven't had a nightmare since then. The speaker also told me that God was taking me through a season of testing and that he saw me going through the furnace and then coming out the other end as pure as gold. He added that God was encouraging me to stay the course since I was (and still am) walking the narrow road of life with God. His prophetic words rang true and after the impactful one-on-one, I decided it was time for me to start attending church again.

I checked out a Chinese church that my roommate recommended, and I was a bit skeptical because I had a lot of negative experiences with Chinese people (even though I am Chinese). It was a typical church service, but at the end of it I saw someone getting slain in the Spirit (falling down under the power of God). While I was watching with curiosity, I started to get an intense feeling inside of me that became unbearable and my thoughts weren't in English anymore; they were in my prayer language. I bolted out of the church as fast as I could and I only felt normal again after I was quite a distance away from the church.

That experience freaked me out. I continued my search to find another church, but at the other churches I didn't feel anything or hear God speak to me. I finally decided to go back to the Chinese church because it was the only church where I felt something, although it wasn't pleasant.

At the Chinese church, I was completely miserable. It wasn't because the people were not nice. Actually, they were very hospitable toward me and they changed my view about Chinese people in general. I simply knew in my spirit that I wasn't going to make any friends there. I faithfully attended even though I didn't connect with anyone there, and after about a year and a half I felt God lead me to go to another church. It felt like a test from God to see if I would be faithful to go to whatever church He wanted me to go to, regardless of how I felt about it.

During my time at the Chinese church, two significant events happened. One was when someone came back from an outside conference and gave me a book. The book was about becoming a seer. I asked her why she was giving me the book, and she just said it was a popular book about seeing in the spirit realm and she felt like God wanted me to read it. I looked at the book questioningly, since I was not a seer and had no interest in seeing in the spirit realm. I of course said, "Thank you," when she gave me the book, but I had no intention of ever reading it.

Another time one of the elders came over to talk to me at church and said that I was going to be a seer. I don't remember his exact words because I was too upset at the time. I immediately responded by saying, "Hell, no!" and then quickly walked away from him. He looked kind of amused at my offense. He was known to be a seer by everyone at church, so his words had weight to them.

I absolutely did not want to be a seer. I was completely against the thought of it because I had experienced so much spiritual warfare in my past. Why would I want to see demons in the spirit realm? Seeing would bring everything I felt and dreamed into 3D. Fortunately, later God completely changed my view about the seeing gift.

I was still continuing on my journey to feel God's

presence, but I wasn't receiving the breakthrough that I was really craving. The breakthrough that I wanted was to feel God's presence all the time, like I did during the two weeks following the retreat. That's not to say I didn't feel God's presence at all. I did feel God's presence at random times and when I prayed in tongues at the top of my lungs, but it wasn't continuous. I knew there was a blockage.

I suspected that the blockage was that I was afraid of getting slain in the Spirit. I knew that I was slain after Pastor Gab placed his hand on my head, which freaked me out afterwards. Ever since then, I would shake violently every time someone laid hands on me to pray for me. One day at the Chinese church a lot of people were falling down from the Spirit when the speaker was laying hands on them. When the speaker finally came to lay hands on me, I was shaking violently and had my defenses up. I didn't get slain at that moment because God was being a gentlemen and He wasn't going to do anything to me if I was that afraid.

My roommate at that time was going to a new church in the East Bay and I noticed a huge change in her. She moved in the Spirit more, which peaked my interest in her new church. The first time I went to the new church with her, I was blown away by how freely the Holy Spirit moved there, but I wasn't going to change churches until I had confirmation from God.

One night I was hanging out with my friend and suddenly his tone changed. He started firmly saying, "You know what

God is asking you to do to get closer to Him. Why don't you just do it?" It was obvious that God was speaking through him, because he had no way of knowing what God had been telling me to do, and we weren't even talking about that topic. This was the confirmation I needed to move forward to get closer to God.

I knew I had to get slain again. God highlighted a leader from my roommate's new church as a potential person I could get prayer from, so I attended the church a second time. That night the leader was giving out prophetic words to the congregation. He asked, "Does anyone want to receive God's powerful presence?" No one raised their hands, which I didn't understand. Who wouldn't want to receive God's presence? I wanted to feel God's presence, but I didn't raise my hand because I didn't like drawing attention to myself, plus I was a new attender and I wasn't feeling that confident.

Then the leader proceeded to call me out to stand up. When I stood up, he said to my roommate who was sitting next to me, "Stand up. You want it too." It was only my roommate and me that were called out to stand up. He asked certain people to come pray for us and he came over to my roommate to personally pray for her. My roommate got slain in the Spirit, which honestly freaked me out, but I no longer wanted fear to control me. I was asking God to please help me, and when the leader came to pray for me, I fell down in the Spirit for the first time in my life.

While I was still on the floor, another leader gave me a word saying that I was like a piece of toast that finally popped out from the toaster oven, and a whole new level was opening up to me spiritually. Then he blessed me on my journey. My life from that point on has never been the same.

After that day, I fell out in the Spirit almost every day for a couple of months. Someone didn't even have to lay hands on me and I would fall. Every time I felt the Spirit of God strongly on me I would instantly be on the floor, which I found to be completely annoying. I had so many bruises on my body, especially on my knees. I was also experiencing other manifestations like spasmic shaking of my body, random sensations on different body parts, and a constant burning sensation on both of my hands. I also would see random bursts of images in my mind when I prayed for people, but I really started seeing after a conference that my roommate's church was going to be hosting. I had very high expectations for it.

At the conference, during one session we were told that none of the speakers onstage were going to lay hands on anyone. The speaker leading the session said that God was already there and all we had to do was receive an impartation in the room. I was speaking in tongues and focusing on God with my hands turned upwards to receive when I saw a shadow walk by me. I asked God in my head, "What was that?" Then I saw more shadows walking toward me until they were standing in front of me. One of them touched both of my forearms. I felt like I was being embraced by all of them, and then I went down on the floor again. This was only my second encounter in the spirit realm (I considered my first encounter to be when I met God in my Cadillac dream).

The first night after the conference, I had a night terror. They continued to terrorize me for many months until I found out how to deal with them directly, so they wouldn't come back again. I believe the reason why the enemy was attacking me was to make me afraid of seeing into the spirit realm. I knew I had received an impartation of seeing at the conference, and it catapulted me into the start of my journey of seeing every day.

Besides my Chinese church, I started attending my roommate's church as well, because of my experience being slain in the Spirit at her church and visions I was having, which caused an increasing strain on me. Eventually, I knew I had to decide to go to just one church. Long story short, it got resolved one day when I heard God tell me that I need to stay at my roommate's church to help a new friend in her future ministry. I left the Chinese church out of obedience to God, and He blessed me with a couple of new good friends from my roommate's church.

The visions that I had after the conference came at random times. I couldn't pinpoint when I was going to have my next vision. I knew when the presence of God was strong in the room or if I started praying at the top of my lungs going for the more of God, the likelihood for me to get a vision was high, so I started going to every Spirit-filled worship session that I possibly could.

Most of my visions were glimpses of Heaven and sometimes I saw angels playing in the background, but since they were so far away, they were blurry. When I did see angels up close, they looked like shadows who interacted with me. I had to ask God every time that I saw a shadow whether it was an angel or if was the Holy Spirit. I definitely didn't have to ask God if the shadow was evil or not, because I didn't feel the peace of God at all during those visions.

Eventually, I didn't see angels as shadows anymore. Instead I saw them with wings or no wings wearing white flowing robes, but I still couldn't make out their faces very clearly. Even to this day, I think I have only seen one angel's face clearly. It happened when I saw a blue outline of an angel looking directly at me and helping me pray for a friend who needed healing. After the angel left, my friend was completely healed. Now I mostly see angels in a golden hue, but other people may tell you that they see angels in various colors.

I also began seeing visions of Jesus, but they were few and far between the other visions that I was seeing. I would only see parts of His body sometimes and the details of His appearance seemed fuzzy. When I did see Jesus, I always had an intense reaction. I could be feeling extremely happy or be crying uncontrollably or be shaking like crazy. If I was standing when I saw Jesus, I had a hard time staying upright, which would stop the vision, so I tried to sit down if I suspected that I was about to recieve a vision.

Seeing Jesus sporadically was a driving force behind doing everything I could to have more visions. Despite having all these visions, my heart's desire was still to feel God's presence every moment of my life. I knew that working full time with a three hour commute was preventing me from getting my heart's desire, but I still had to make a living. I could only devote two days a week for God, which made me very sad. However, God knew the desire of my heart and He made a way for me to go to Bethel School of Supernatural Ministry in Redding, California.

My Journey
To Bethel

Before I even applied and was accepted to Bethel School of Supernatural Ministry (BSSM) in Redding, California, I bought a house there. Buying a house in Redding was all God's idea and certainly was not mine. I never imagined owning a house in Redding of all places. I didn't want to move to Redding since I had lived in the Bay Area for most of my life. I didn't have anything against Redding; it was just so different from any place that I had ever lived.

One day in 2015 I drove someone from the Bay Area back to her home in Redding. She was a real estate agent, so I talked to her about home prices in Redding and she sent me some listings of homes that were on the market. One home in particular was highlighted to me. I asked her about it and she asked if I wanted to start the process of buying. I said, "No," because my debt to income ratio wasn't where it needed to be. I happened to know this because I worked at a bank at the time.

Nevertheless, I sent in a request for a mortgage pre-approval with my company thinking I would be declined. Shockingly, I got approved! Had my co-workers not known me personally, I think I would have been declined.

We went into escrow on the home and the inspection reports came back with $4,000 worth of repairs that needed to be done. I thought, "Surely God wouldn't want me to live in a house that is falling apart. I guess I won't be moving to Redding after all." I asked if the owners would be willing to fix everything on the report, doubting they would agree. To my amazement, they agreed to fix everything. The house even closed on my ex-partner's birthday, which I felt was God's kindness to flip what I had seen as a bad day into a good day going forward.

I had always wanted to own a single family detached home, but detached homes in the Bay Area were out of my price range, so I settled for a condo. I was working as many hours as possible to pay off the condo quickly. My plan was that once I finished paying off the condo, I would get a tenant to rent out my extra room and I would quit my job and live off the rental income. Two years after I closed on my home in Redding, my dream became a reality. God told me that if I sold my condo from the Bay Area (which I had been renting out), it would pay off my new home in Redding.

My house in Redding is a total gift from God! By His grace I had saved enough money for the down payment and the profit from selling my condo paid for the rest two years later. God gave me one of my heart's secret desires and He was about to do it again.

I knew that God wanted me to live in Redding since He orchestrated my housing, and I also knew that He wanted me to attend BSSM. I applied to the school, and of course, I was accepted. However, too many changes in my life were happening all at once, and I was stressed out about everything. A month before I was scheduled to leave the Bay Area, I received a prophetic word that reassured me that moving to Redding was the best decision for me. A woman I never met said, "I heard the words, 'I [God] am bringing you into a new season of happiness, a season of joy, and a season of answered dreams.' He's going to bring you into a season where He's going to talk to you every day. God says, 'Come and dance with me. It's going to be glorious and grand.'" This word was exactly what I needed to hear. It kept me motivated to continue staying on course, even though the transition had been very hard on me.

I began school in the fall of 2016, and it was indeed a glorious and grand adventure with God and my fellow students. During my time at BSSM, I listened to two significant teachings that impacted how I engaged in the spiritual realm. I still use the principles from these two teachings in my personal life today.

The first teaching happened when I took a prophetic ministry training class. On the first day of class, we were asked to find a partner and take time to ask God what He wanted to say to the person in front of us. While I was asking God, I felt in my spirit that this was the ticket to get words of knowledge and prophetic words for people. I suddenly realized that God had just given me another one of my heart's desires.

It had always been a desire of mine to give people words from God, but when I had asked prophetic people how to do this, they would just tell me to say anything that popped in my head, believing it would be an inspired thought from God. Their advice did not help me. I also read numerous books about prophecy, which didn't help either. After a while, I just gave up trying to learn, and I thought that it wasn't a gift that I was supposed to have. To say I was excited to have the key to give words of knowledge and prophetic words is an understatement.

I started to practice on people whenever I could. I discovered that when I asked God what He wanted to say to people, sometimes words would get jumbled up in my head because of my dyslexia, so I had to modify what I was taught in class. Since I'm more of a visual learner, I would imagine Jesus in front of the person that I wanted to give a word to, and then ask Jesus what He wanted to say to that person. Then He would show me a picture. Only after I got a clear image in my mind and I asked Jesus what the image meant would I release what I felt He was saying.

When I first started giving words, it took some time for me to actually see a picture and then get the interpretation for someone. My speed only picked up with practice. Nowadays, most of the time, I can just look at someone and an image will instantly pop in my head without me imagining Jesus, but I still use the same technique of imagining Jesus and asking Him what He wants to say to the person when I don't get a picture instantaneously.

Words of knowledge and prophetic words may seem totally unrelated to seeing in the spirit realm, but how I learned to give words jumpstarted my journey into seeing every day. I thought to myself, if I can see what God wants to relay to someone else, why can't I do the same for myself? In response to my own question, I started to imagine myself being in front of Jesus and asking Him what He wanted to say to me during my prayer times. This question made a huge difference. The numbers of visions I received increased dramatically. I saw in the spirit realm more consistently, and I saw Jesus more often as well. I believe the reason was because I was focused on seeing Jesus or what Jesus was showing me, instead of only asking for more of God.

Another practice that increased my visions was how I

prayed. When I started BSSM I was still praying the same way that I prayed before, which was screaming at the top of my lungs in tongues while being completely focused on asking for more of God's presence. I learned in school that this was called travailing. I couldn't really travail while I was in school, since it would have freaked people out. So, instead, I would just speak in tongues quietly, but with intensity, while asking God for more of Him and imagining Jesus in front of me at the same time. This way proved to be just as successful, if not more so, than travailing. I could pray longer and also receive more visions. After this discovery, I would only travail if my quiet way of praying didn't seem to elicit a breakthrough and I really wanted to get God's attention.

The second transformational teaching happened when a leader who is a prophet spoke to our class about the gift of seeing. He talked about how anyone can see in the spirit realm and how everyone gets visions. He added that people often overlook visions when they see them. Visions, he said, only last about three seconds. They can easily be missed if you're not paying attention, or you may dismiss them as random thoughts. He said the next time we see an image randomly pop in our head, we should grab hold of it and start asking God questions about it. When I started doing what he instructed, I received even more visions. These visions would often occur outside of my prayer time, which made me aware that God spoke to me more frequently than I realized.

These two teachings (asking Jesus what He wants to say to you when you imagine Him in front of you, and asking Jesus questions about random visions) showed me that anyone can receive the gift of seeing through practice, and that the gift doesn't come solely through impartation or the laying on of hands. If I needed to see something in the spirit realm and I wasn't receiving any information, I would often use one or both of these techniques.

My pursuit of God's presence never stopped, even when God gave me an upgrade in my seer gift. When my visions increased because of the techniques I learned from school, I really started going after seeing Jesus in my visions every day, which I still find very ironic since initially I didn't want the seer gift at all. As I was seeing more and more of Jesus in my visions, I got to know Jesus more intimately. I got to know Him as my friend.

As with all friendship, we started to converse back and forth with each other. It was not a one-sided pursuit of me going after Jesus; He would go after me as well. It didn't matter what time of day it was or where I was when I would encounter Jesus. I even saw Jesus smiling at me while I was in the middle of taking a shower!

I was able to discover different sides of Jesus' personality as I encountered Him in visions. I saw how kind Jesus is, especially when I was suffering from bouts of depression. Another side I saw was His sassiness and quick wit. I'm very sassy when I talk to Jesus, and Jesus is sassy back to me. Jesus is also very humorous and fun, which I sometimes didn't appreciate because I tend to be more serious. There were other sides of Jesus' personality that I experienced too.

People also tend to do things together when they are friends. Jesus started to interject Himself when He wanted to have a face-to-face encounter with someone I was praying for or talking to and He also started to highlight random people for me to pray for, which made me very uncomfortable at times. Sometimes I would know what to pray for when I approached someone, but most of the time I had no clue, so I simply had to ask the person if they needed prayer for anything. People would either stare at me blankly or they would be happy that God highlighted them to me. No matter what the outcome was, I was excited to pray for anyone that was highlighted to me because I wanted to co-labor with God.

Partnering with God and praying for strangers can be a lot fun. It enabled me to see how God moves and experience things that I would not normally get to experience. This doesn't mean that I was always on target when someone was highlighted to me. Sometimes I didn't approach someone for one reason or another. And other times they would not want prayer or wouldn't have any visible reaction to what I prayed. As I prayed for more and more people, I saw and felt how much love God truly has for His people, which changed how I felt toward people as well.

Beyond changing my heart toward people, God answered my prayer to be able to go into His presence anytime I wanted. I simply called on His name in my mind, and I would be in His presence instantly. I believe this happened because I had built a relationship with God. Other people may get into God's presence differently than me, which is just fine. God can encounter His people in numerous ways. This is not to say that I stopped praying because I didn't need to pray anymore in order to feel His presence. I still pray every day because I know that prayers are powerful and I want God to hear my prayers.

Nowadays, I interact with Jesus in the spiritual realm almost every day. I can say that I actually have a relationship with Jesus. I do interact with Father God, Holy Spirit, and angels, but I interact with Jesus the most. I get different types of visions when I'm praying for other people, but the visions that I mostly get for myself have Jesus in them.

It became apparent to me that my visions were very different from other seer's visions when I started talking about what I see. I wondered why I didn't see the same kinds of visions as other seers, and after contemplating how we only prophesy in part based on 1 Corinthians 13, I concluded that we only see in part as well.

A common question people ask me is whether there are angels in the room. I honestly say that I don't know, and I don't care to know. Angels are important to the Kingdom, but they are not to be worshiped. I worship God and not angels. However, I do see angels quite often. If I see them near me when I'm praying for someone, I will ask them to come help me. I often see myself flying alongside them or standing next to them with wings on my back because God sees me as an agent for Him. For the most part, I see them worshiping God.

Another common question that people ask me is whether I see God in nature, and I would tell them, "No." I don't worship nature or objects. Occasionally I have seen people in the spirit realm enjoying themselves in front of a sunrise or a sunset, and I would think to myself, "That's a cool vision," but nothing beyond that. I'm a city girl. I would rather be inside, in a comfortable temperature controlled environment, over being outside any day. I believe the reason why I mainly see Jesus in my visions is because I was praying for years to have more of God's presence. I can't say that I won't grow in appreciation for visions with angels or nature or other things, because my visions are constantly evolving and God can change my perception on anything.

People often ask me how to become more prophetic or get certain spiritual gifts. My answer is simple: always obey God and die to yourself. This raises other questions in their minds, the first being, "How does obeying relate to getting spiritual gifts?" When you obey God, you are letting God direct your steps and you are walking alongside God. No one can walk alongside God without being obedient. The more you obey God, the more God will come to trust you, and as a result you'll become closer to Him. When you are in a close relationship with God you will come to know Him as a supernatural God, so signs and wonders will naturally follow you. My life has become very supernatural, to the point where I have seen signs and wonders almost every day.

The second thing that people often ask me is, "If I have free will, don't I have a choice whether or not to obey God? If I choose not to obey God, won't God still love me?" God did give us free will to either follow Him or not to follow Him. It is true that God will still love you no matter what, even if you decide to disobey Him, but the following questions come to mind. Didn't Jesus die for you? Are you willing to die for Him? Do you trust God to direct your path in life? Do you trust that God has the best for you? Are you a true follower of Christ? If you answered "no" to these questions, you are basically saying that you don't trust God and that you don't love Him.

Furthermore, when people choose not to obey God, they are essentially giving their blessings away to someone else. If God asks us to do something and we choose not to do it, God will ask someone else. If we keep saying "no" to God, He will eventually stop asking us. The people who say "yes" to God will be used mightily by God and will receive untold blessings.

The third thing that people ask me is, "If I do the two

techniques in this book, will I be able to see into the spirit realm without doing anything else?" Essentially they are telling me that they want to see in the spirit realm without obeying God. To answer the question, yes I believe that anyone can eventually see in the spirit realm with the techniques shown in this book with enough diligence and practice. When they actually start seeing, they will get to know God's character more, which hopefully will inspire them to get closer to Him and to obey Him because of their love relationship with Him.

There are several reasons why I personally obey God always. When I obey God, I'm telling God that I love Him and that I want to be in a relationship with Him. I believe you show that you love someone by making sacrifices and by doing things for them. Another reason is because I know that God is powerful, and that He is always right. Even before I became a Christian, I obeyed God when He told me to go to Livingwater Church because I was afraid to disobey the all powerful, all knowing God. I'm happy that I did obey Him then, since I most likely wouldn't be where I am now had I not obeyed Him.

I don't ever regret obeying God, even when it has been difficult at times, because the outcomes have always been good for me. Even when I'm upset or don't agree with what God is asking me to do, I always end up obeying since I know that God is a lot smarter than me. I come to find out in the end, time and time again, that God is always right, and that

I have a limited understanding of the whole picture. Obeying God has always benefited me.

Living a life of obedience is not easy. Oftentimes, I'm misunderstood. Some decisions that I made in the past seemed foolish to people at first, but later on they came to see the decisions were the best for me. For example, many were puzzled or shocked when I first told them I was going to quit my job and move to Redding and attend a ministry school. But when people find out what my life is like in Redding now, they completely change their tune.

Obeying God and living a life of purity has sometimes meant I don't fit in with certain people because I don't participate in things like drinking alcohol or watching certain things. I choose to live a life of purity because I don't want to miss any opportunity to hear God speak to me, knowing that sin of any kind could block me from hearing His voice accurately. I know that the road to life with God is narrow and that many people will not be traveling with me on that road, but I'm more than okay with that. He is my great reward!

It's not always easy when God tests my faith through obedience. A major test was being led to attend the Chinese church and then my roommate's church, even when I had reservations about both of them. The ultimate test was when I felt God wanted me to leave my whole life behind and sell everything to move to Redding. My life in Redding was rocky for the first few years because I was so homesick, but my life since then has been so blessed. I have never been this content in my whole life. I would never have experienced this happiness if I had not been faithful obeying God every step of the way.

God rewards obedience. God has rewarded me with so many of my heart's desires, and He has graced me with gifts and spiritual gifts that I never asked or prayed for. I believe that it is always in our best interest to obey God, whether it makes sense to us or not.

DIFFERENT WAYS OF SEEING

There are many different ways of seeing in the spirit realm and I want to share unique encounters that I have had with the seer gift. Perhaps some of these stories will inspire you to remember ways that you have seen in the spirit realm and open you up to seeing in new ways. When I talk about seeing, that not only includes seeing with my mind's eye, but also sensing things on my body, which sometimes causes physical reactions (also known as manifestations). The ways I share about seeing are by no means inclusive, since God can talk to each of us differently. In fact, I hope that God speaks to you outside of the box of what you consider normal and outside of what I share here! These encounters are not in any particular order. Let's begin.

RECEIVING GUIDANCE

Before I became a Christian I was a huge fan of a TV show that featured aliens, and I owned the DVD set of the whole series. I didn't want to get rid of it because it wasn't cheap and I wanted to watch it again, but I wasn't sure whether I should, so I asked God if it would be okay to re-watch it. While I was asking God, I was staring at the DVD set on top of the dresser, and then I saw black smoke emerging from it. Obviously, the answer was, "No."

SEEING SCARS ON JESUS' BODY

I was talking with a friend about how Jesus was always happy and smiling when I saw Him. My friend asked me if I ever saw the scars on His body. I was taken aback by his question because Jesus' body had always seemed flawless to me. Then I started to ask myself if Jesus' body had scars. The next thing I knew I was in the spirit realm looking at the numerous cuts on one of Jesus' forearms that were old and faded, but still very visible. I knew that these scars covered His whole body. I was shocked since I had never noticed the scars on Jesus' body before. Jesus was smiling at me when I was looking at His forearm. I felt Him telling me that He suffered dearly to show His love for us.

EXPERIENCING SHAKING

A manifestation of shaking happened every time I felt God's presence, which could be annoying at times when I needed my hands to be steady. Sometimes, the shaking could even be dangerous, like when I was getting my hair curled by my hairdresser. Luckily, she didn't burn me, which we joked about at the time. I asked God, "What's with the shaking? Why does this happen to me?" He chose to answer me with two different humorous visions. In one vision, I saw Jesus throwing lightning bolts at me from Heaven. Every time a lightning bolt hit me, I would shake. In another vision, Jesus had a bow and arrow aimed at me. Every arrow had a single red heart as the tip, like cupid's arrow. I would shake every time an arrow of God's love struck me.

LAUGHING UNCONTROLLABLY

While I was in a small group meeting for BSSM, I started to laugh uncontrollably, but there was seemingly nothing around me that was making me laugh. Then I saw myself as an unclothed baby. Jesus had a single white feather in His hand that He was tickling me with continuously. I felt Jesus' joy when He was making me laugh.

Feeling a Weight

I was talking to a friend when I saw a tall blue outline of an angel appear behind him. The angel placed its left hand on my friend's left shoulder, and I asked my friend if he felt a weight on his left shoulder. He said, "Yes." As soon as my friend said, "Yes," the angel vanished.

Feeling Sensations

I often feel sensations on different parts of my body. The key to knowing what is happening is to ask God. As I was writing this book, I felt something consistently on my lower back, and at times it was distracting. One time God told me that angels were massaging my back because I had been having back pain from sitting too long. A few days later when I asked God about it again, He gave me a different answer. This time I saw a myriad of angels behind my back cheering me on to write. It was quite difficult for me to write because of my struggle with dyslexia, so this vision motivated me to keep on writing.

Another time I felt something in the center of my upper back and I saw huge white wings being inserted into my back. To me this signified how God saw me like a messenger for Him.

Here is a list of what other sensations meant to me as God showed me visions to accompany the sensations.

- *Dripping on my head* = An angel was pouring a clay pitcher full of oil onto my head, which was dripping onto both of my hands. I felt that God was anointing me and that I was supposed to bless people with the overflow of oil.

- *Tingling on my head* = Jesus was pulling things that looked like wires out of my head and reknitting them back into my head. He was rewiring my thinking.

- *Feeling weight on my shoulders* = A heavy robe was draped over my shoulders. In various visions the robe and trim were different colors. This was to remind me of my royal identity.

- *Feeling weight on my head* = I saw myself with either a white sheer veil or a flower crown on my head while I was wearing a white flowing dress. I'm reminded on how God saw me as the bride of Christ.

- *Feeling a tight band around my head* = A crown was placed on top of my head. This was to remind me of my position and identity in Christ.

- *Feeling weight on my hands while praying* = I saw myself with either an open book or a sword laid across my hands. If I there was a book, the book contained stories about me and the great things that I had done or would do for God. If there was a sword, I would often see myself using it skillfully to slay a dragon or a dark spirit that was coming against me. This was

God's way of telling me that I have the power, given by God, to combat any darkness that comes my way.

- ***Squeezing of my right shoulder*** = Jesus was squeezing my right shoulder to let me know that He's there for me and that I'm not alone in this world.
- ***Heat on my hands*** = I saw balls of fire on both my hands. Every time I felt heat on my hands, I would ask God to direct me to who needed prayer at that moment either for healing or for feeling the presence of God with the laying on of hands.

SEEING SOMEONE ELSE HAVE AN ENCOUNTER

The presence of God was really strong at an event and during one session when we were all praying, I felt that my friend, who was next to me, was having an encounter. I looked in my friend's direction, and he was in fact in the middle of an encounter. I saw, in my mind's eye, tiny gold particles flowing all around him, and I also saw Jesus in front of him. Jesus noticed that I saw Him. He was smiling as He turned His head toward me, and then He turned His attention back to my friend. My friend was happily crying with his eyes closed and both of his hands raised praising God. Jesus was telling my friend how much He loved him and that He was very proud of him.

PRAYING FOR HEALING

A man asked me to pray for his hurt knee. I laid my hand on his knee and I was waiting for God to tell me when to remove my hand. I was thinking that I was waiting a little too long, so I asked God, "What's going on?" Then I saw Jesus in the distance laughing and dancing, which annoyed me because He was goofing off and not helping me pray. Jesus continued to laugh and dance even though I asked Him to please come and help me. Instead of helping me, He led me to give a long prophetic word while my hand was still on the man's knee. After I was done giving the word, I was finally able to take my hand off his knee. The man said that his knee felt much better, and that the word I gave him blessed him deeply. Out of all the healing stories that I could have shared, I decided to include this one because it illustrates how God cares about people's hearts just as much as He cares about healing their ailments. When I pray for healing, I usually engage in the spiritual realm to see what God wants to do, which greatly benefits the person that I'm praying for.

SEEING PEOPLE'S HOMES

In the story above when I was praying for the man's knee to be healed, I went into a vision where I saw the layout of his living room and other small details about his home. I mentioned that his living room was minimally decorated and there were a lot of magnets on his refrigerator, which he confirmed were true. At other times I saw a lady's kitchen, which was narrow in size, and I saw another lady's living room where she had knickknacks from China displayed. I don't ask to see people's homes, but Jesus decides what He wants to show me.

SEEING CAN MAKE AN IMPACT

One Saturday there was a guest in the Healing Rooms who wanted to receive prayers from as many people as possible. My friend asked me to give him a word and I said, "No. You have the Holy Spirit living inside of you, so you can give him a word." My friend unfortunately wasn't going to take "no" for an answer, so he grabbed my hand and placed it on the guest. Immediately, I had a vision about the guest, so I ended up praying for him. I gave the guest a word saying he was very hungry for God, and that he had been studious in reading the Word in order to connect with God more.

The guest didn't seem very receptive to what I saying at first. It was only after I told him that I saw him reading the Word at a large brown table with items placed neatly on it, that he seemed more accepting of what I was saying. I found out later from my friend that everyone before me had essentially said what I had said about him wanting more of God, so the guest probably thought that I had overheard them and was just repeating what they were saying about him. However, when I shared about seeing the brown table, it made the prophetic word more impactful because the picture obviously came from God.

SEEING THROUGH TOUCH

In the story above, my friend knew that if I were to lay my hands on someone, I would most likely get a vision and a word for that person. He knew this because it happened when he and I had prayed together before in the Healing Rooms. One time we were ministering to a lady, and I was letting my friend pray for her by himself. My friend saw that I wasn't doing anything, so he motioned for me to step in and pray too. I wasn't getting anything from God for her, but as soon as I held her hand, I saw a couple of things about her and then I shared what I saw and I prayed for her.

Laying on of hands is a way to connect to someone's spirit easier. Most of the time this is a positive thing, but it can be a negative when I see something that's upsetting. I learned this the hard way when a group of us were ministering to a guy during my first mission trip. Once my hand touched his back, I saw how horrible his past was. Everyone in his life was calling him names and making him cry, which made me want to cry. Ever since that time, I've been more discerning on who I lay hands on, which is a practice that anyone who's sensitive to the spirit realm should do.

When I have a check in my spirit (i.e. an uneasy feeling about a particular person), that is how I know whether I need to ask God if the person is safe for me to lay hands on. This is not always possible when I have to lay hands on a room full of people when I am serving on a ministry team. In this case, after I am done serving I will pray to keep myself filled up with God's presence. And if I do see something disturbing while laying my hands on people I will ask God to come into my vision, which I'll expound upon in the chapter on spiritual attacks.

SEEING MANIFESTATIONS IN THE NATURAL

While I was praying for my friend over the phone, I saw a vision of him kneeling with one knee on the ground while God was knighting him. When I told my friend what I saw after I finished praying, he told me during the time of my vision he was lying on the sofa and his 4-year-old son came toward him, kissed him on the forehead, and then walked away.

Another time I was inside my friend's house when my friend discovered that her front door was left wide open. She was certain that she had shut the door. She kept asking everyone if we felt there was anything significant about the door being open. I just thought that someone must have left the door open by accident, but since my friend was so persistent in asking, I asked God about the door and I saw a shadow of an angel burst through the door and leave it wide open. After I shared that, my friend's husband added that he understood the purpose of the angel's visit to their home. I realized at that moment that I shouldn't dismiss things so easily because there might be a supernatural reason for things happening in the natural.

HAVING SHARED VISIONS

One day my friend got an image for me while we were talking. He saw a key and was telling me about the importance of the key in my life, but he didn't say anything at all about what the key looked like. I told him that the key was gray in color to let him know that I could see the key too. When we started to talk about the physical aspects of the key, we found out that we were both seeing the same type of key. It's really cool when I do get to share the same vision with someone because each of us can see different aspects of the exact same thing.

SEEING DEAD PEOPLE

A friend who I hadn't talked to in a while texted me to ask me to pray for her mother and tell her what I saw. I texted her back and told her some things about her mother's personality that God showed me. Then she texted me to tell me that her mother had actually died recently, which blew me away because from the vision I had, I thought her mother was still living. This wasn't the first time that I wasn't able to tell if a person I was praying for was still living or not.

There were times when people showed me pictures of their loved ones who had passed away, and asked me if I saw anything in the spirit realm about them. Every time I have been asked that, I have seen their loved ones as very active in my visions, as though they were still alive. I wouldn't have known the difference if they were dead or alive. I believe the reason why is because when we die, we are not really dead since we are just moving to a new home. Our spirits either go back home to Heaven or to hell, depending on whether we chose to follow Jesus while we were still living on earth. This is my personal belief and is not based on any theological studies. I have heard stories of people being able to see and interact with dead people in their new homes in Heaven, but I have not personally experienced this yet.

SEEING SPIRITS CONTROL PEOPLE'S WORDS

I mentioned a story earlier about my friend who suddenly changed his tone and told me I needed to do what God was telling me to do to get closer to Him. We hadn't talked about this before, and my friend had no way of knowing what God had been talking to me about. As I was staring at my friend's face when he was speaking these words, I saw an angel in my friend's body with its wings expanded and Heaven as the backdrop. The Heaven I saw was sunny with green plants and different colored flowers everywhere. It felt as though the angel was talking to me directly from Heaven through my friend. I could also feel my friend's sense of pride from being used by God to talk to me, and his willingness to allow the angel to control his mouth.

Another time when I visited my friend I felt I needed to hold his hand. I suddenly became very captivated with my friend's eyes. He started tearing up, which I had never seen him do before. His eyes became like Jesus' eyes when he spoke and said that I should not have thoughts about myself that don't align with what Jesus thinks of me. I saw Jesus in my friend's body while he was speaking to me.

Dark spirits can also talk through people. The company I used to work for was planning to have a huge Halloween celebration. I did not want any part of it because I believe it is possible to open up a door for dark spirits to come in by celebrating Halloween. I took Halloween day off, and two days later my boss called me into her office. She said that a couple of people complained that I was sitting cross-legged during a meeting, which they said looked unprofessional. I told her that I wouldn't do it again. My boss sympathized with me saying she was surprised that people even noticed the way that I was sitting. Then out of the blue she said, "You're not a leader." I didn't know how to respond to her. I was thinking, "Why would you even say that to me? I am only an analyst and no one reports to me." I had to agree with her because she was my boss, and then I left her office.

Later that night, I was crying in bed. No one had complained about me before the Halloween celebration, and I felt like it wasn't fair that dark spirits were influencing people at work to come against me. I went into a vision while I was still crying, where I saw myself lying on red checkered picnic blanket underneath a tree being spooned by an angel shadow who was trying to comfort me. Honestly, I didn't feel that much comfort from the angel. God knew that I needed more comfort, so I went into a second vision where I saw my boss sitting at her desk and a dark shadow standing next to her controlling her mouth. I finally felt comfort in knowing that it wasn't my boss who was speaking to me. God said, "You are a leader and the enemy always likes to contradict my words." I learned that I need to discern what spirit is operating when someone says things that contradict what God has said about me. I also learned how to remove the dark spirits from my workplace, which I'll discuss later.

When I say that a dark spirit is speaking through someone, it doesn't mean that the person is possessed by a demon. It simply means they are allowing a demon to influence them by some type of agreement. For the three encounters I mentioned above, all three people who spoke were fully aware of what they were saying. My boss looked instantly regretful after she told me that I wasn't a leader, and she chose to never mention it again. We do have a choice regarding which spirits we partner with when we speak. Next time you open your mouth to say something, ask yourself why you want to say it. Is what you're about to say coming from your spirit, God's Spirit, or other dark spirits?

SEEING PEOPLE PRAY

When people say they are going to pray for me, I usually think they are simply saying it to be nice and are not actually going to do it. But when my friend told me that he was going to pray for me, he meant it. I would be doing something and then suddenly, I would see an image of my friend praying for me. The image would keep repeating in my mind's eye until my friend was done praying for me. I would often ask my friend later if he did in fact pray for me, and he would always say, "Yes." I would also ask him if he prayed for me at a certain time and he would say, "No," half of the time, so that was a bit of a mystery.

I have another friend who is a prayer warrior and she would often tell me that she prayed for me. So far not once have I ever seen her in the spirit realm praying for me. I can't explain why God decided to show me one friend praying for me and not another.

One night I was winding down to go to sleep when I

suddenly started thinking about my friend and felt concerned for him. I saw him in my mind's eye praying earnestly. I couldn't shake my growing concern for him, even after I prayed a general prayer for him, so I decided to send him a message. It was 2:00am and I didn't want to wake him up in case he was sleeping, so I decided to send him a Facebook message since he normally only checked his messages during the day. In my message I said I felt God told me that he was awake and I asked him if he was okay. Surprisingly, he responded back within a few minutes telling me that he was awake and he was praying to God late that night. It was no accident that my friend saw my message, because God wanted to let him know that his prayers were indeed heard. I was thankful that God used me to bless and encourage my friend.

SEEING PEOPLE'S PHYSICAL FEATURES

I'm often asked while serving in the Healing Rooms to intercede for guests' family members who couldn't be there with them. If I don't know what the family member looks like, I have to ask God to help me so I can do my usual technique of imagining the person in front of Jesus and asking Jesus what He wants to say to that person. Most often, an image of the person will form in my mind's eye and then I can start asking Jesus things about the person. In one case I was able to share with a woman that her brother was skinnier than her, significantly taller than her, and he liked wearing colorful clothing. She confirmed those were true statements. I have seen time and time again how God honors what people ask for by giving me these pictures to encourage them that God sees their loved ones.

There is one thing that I don't normally share about people who I've seen in the spirit realm, and that is their hairstyle or hair color. I've often been told that I was wrong when I shared this information and I've also realized that the images of people I know and have seen in the spirit realm don't necessarily match their appearance in real life. For instance, I've often seen myself as a little girl with long curly black hair, but my hair is somewhat wavy and is mid length. I've also seen my friend as a little boy with short black hair, but in real life my friend is old enough to be my father and his hair is white.

I once told someone that I saw her daughter's hair with purple ends, and the mother told me that they spent all last summer trying to dye her ends purple with no success. In addition, I've learned that people's hairstyles or hair color may change throughout their lifetime, so to save myself from embarrassment, I don't normally share about the appearance of someone's hair unless God specifically tells me to share it.

SEEING HOW OTHER PEOPLE SEE

One time I was asked to give prophetic words to my former church leader's family who was visiting Redding for the day. One of them was the elder who originally prophesied that I would become a seer. I had some reservations about giving him a word since he's a much more advanced seer than I am. At the same time, I was curious and excited about what God wanted to show me about him. When I was standing in front of him, I immediately saw how he sees in the spiritual realm, which was like nothing I had ever seen before. In the vision, the elder could see everything that was happening in the spirit realm in real time. If he turned his head toward a person, he would see a colored aura that outlined their whole body. Or if something appeared to be attached to a person's body, he would know how it would affect the person positively or negatively. My vision only lasted for a minute, but when I saw how the elder sees, it made me realize how limited my visions were and motivated me to seek God for greater depth of the seer gift.

SEEING SIMILAR VISIONS MULTIPLE TIMES

I had a vision that really spoke to me, and I couldn't stop thinking about it. In the vision, I was a shadow sandwiched between two angel shadows. The two angels did not have wings, but they wanted me to feel special, so they gave me large white wings. I felt very loved and honored by them. I wanted something tangible to remember the vision, so I decided to paint it. I painted the background green with colored speckles to represent visions of green grass and flowers I had seen in Heaven. It took me almost two weeks to complete the painting since I wanted the painting to look exactly like my vision. The novelty of the painting wore off when I started receiving other visions, so the painting was stored in my closet for a number of years.

I hadn't thought about the painting in years, until one day it popped into my head as I had a vision of my friend. He was in between two angels that were flying him up to Heaven to meet God. Each angel had an arm wrapped around one of his arms, so all three flew together in a row. He had big white wings placed on him, which he didn't feel comfortable with because they were noticeable. The angels wanted to let him know that he was very special to God. When he finally met up with God, he kept saying that he was just a servant and nothing more.

The painting came to mind again when I was in Mexico on a mission trip and I had two back-to-back visions. In the first vision, my fellow classmate was in between two angels who were helping her joyfully minister to people in different places. This was a stark contrast to the second vision that followed. In the next vision I was in between two angels who each grabbed the tip of my wings and dragged me to different places where

I unhappily ministered to people. Only after seeing how much people were blessed was I happy to go with the angels. After I had these visions I felt motivated to continue to minister to people with joy even though I was tired, and I didn't want to go out to minister anymore.

After having these visions, I hung the painting on my wall and whenever I would look at it and ask God about it, He would speak to me and give me new visions.

PRAYING FOR PEOPLE TO SEE

You may be reading this book and desire to not only get an upgrade in the gift of seeing, but to be able to impart it to others as well. Before you start praying for others to see, make sure that you're at a stage in your life where you're consistently receiving encounters of your own. I believe that it's hard to give something away that you don't have. And if you're a seasoned seer, you'll able to teach people from your experiences and answer questions they may ask.

I never imagined that I would be praying for other people to see in the spirit realm or teaching people how to impart this gift. Praying for people to have encounters was something that I just happened to stumble upon. Early on in my walk with God when I was just learning how to pray for people in general, I was praying for a woman who was in pain because of an autoimmune disease. I held her hands while speaking in tongues and waiting for God to tell me to stop praying. When

I was done, she had tears in her eyes and said she had seen Jesus for the first time! She said she spoke in tongues really fast like me, and then she went into a vision. In the vision she was in a garden following a stream of water. At the end of the stream, she met Jesus and she knew instantly that Jesus healed her. I was amazed that she saw Jesus for the first time, but I didn't think that I had anything to do with it.

Some time later, my friend was experiencing depression, and I went to her house to pray for her. Since I had suffered from depression, I suspected that it might be an attack from the enemy on her mind, and I thought if she could feel the presence of God, the attack might go away. So, I laid my hands on her head to pray for her to feel God's presence and then waited for God to tell me to remove my hands. My friend told me after I was done praying that she saw Jesus and that she felt much better.

These two instances showed me that I have a gift to pray for people to have face-to-face encounters with Jesus. In the beginning, I wasn't confident that I truly had the gift, so I only prayed for friends if I thought they needed an encounter. I would pray for my friends the same way I prayed for myself to encounter God. I would lay my hands on their heads and ask them to imagine Jesus in front of them and to ask Him what He wanted to say to them. After praying this way for a few of my friends and having a 100% success rate, I grew more confident in praying for others to encounter the Lord.

Even as I grew more confident in praying, I also came to understand that Jesus should be the one getting all the credit for showing up. I learned this lesson one day on the side of the road. I drove a friend home and while we were parked on a busy road in front of her apartment, she insisted that I give her a prophetic word. I was so preoccupied with the cars whizzing close to my car that I couldn't prophesy or focus on the images that I was getting for my friend. I decided to pray for her to have an encounter directly with Jesus so He could talk to her. I wasn't sure if it was going to work since I couldn't fix my eyes on Jesus in that moment. I figured my spirit would have to pray for my friend instead of my mind. I laid my hands on her head as usual, and to my surprise, Jesus talked to her! I knew that it wasn't my effort that caused her to encounter Jesus; God did all the work. I am just a vessel that God chooses to use.

My journey of praying for others to see really started to take off after I was on a team praying for a woman for healing. I saw Jesus standing in front of the woman telling me that He wanted to talk to her. I hesitated at first, since I wasn't exactly sure what Jesus wanted me to do and it would be my first time praying for a stranger to have an encounter. Also, the woman wanted healing and not an encounter. Jesus kept looking at me telling me that He really wanted to talk to her and He was waiting for me to take action. I decided to take a chance even though it wasn't how my team was praying for her, and I asked the woman if I could pray for her to have an encounter. She agreed so I placed both my hands on her head and asked her to imagine Jesus in front of her and to ask Him what He wanted to say to her. Honestly, I wasn't sure if Jesus was going to talk to her since I didn't know anything about her history seeing in the spirit realm, but I trusted that God knew. Surprisingly, she told me that Jesus did speak to her.

After that happened, I had a noticeable increase of opportunities to pray for people to have encounters. Jesus started asking me more and more to pray for random strangers. As I did, I observed that those who God highlighted to me were more likely to receive a face-to-face encounter than those who asked me to pray for them to have an encounter. People who approached me would say that they felt the presence of God after I prayed, but they would not always see Jesus. However, if God asked me to pray for someone, it was almost guaranteed that the person would encounter Him.

I had a dream on January 2nd, 2020 and in it I was sitting across from a prominent leader who I didn't know personally. He was talking to me, and while he was talking, I felt the prompting from God to pray for him to have an encounter. I asked him if I could lay my hands on his head, and he said, "No." Because of his firm answer, I held both of his hands and then I started praying for him. I really didn't expect anything to happen since I had never prayed for someone to have an encounter before without touching their head. I believed that laying my hands on people's heads directly affected their minds to see. Both of my hands got really hot when I held his hands, and the heat went away after God told me that He was done. The leader had a surprised look in his eyes, and I knew that he had encountered God.

I asked my prophetic friend the next day what he thought the dream meant, and he told me that God was doing a new thing in my life. He also pointed out that I had been in a rut believing that laying hands on people's heads was the only way they could have an encounter and that God wanted to show me a new way to pray for people.

After the dream, two things changed. The first was how I prayed for people. I had to force myself to not reach for people's heads when I prayed for them. It took me a little while to not automatically pray this way, but now I have had success by simply laying my hands on other parts of people's bodies. God showed me that there is no cookie cutter way to pray.

The second change was the sheer amount of people that God highlighted to me to pray for. Before my dream I would pray for someone to have an encounter every two weeks or so, but after I couldn't go more than a few days without seeing someone who was highlighted. In fact, I no longer had to see Jesus tell me He wanted to talk to someone; I just felt in my spirit that I should pray. I have prayed for so many people now to have encounters that I have lost count!

Given the choice to either pray for someone to have an

encounter or give them a prophetic word, I would choose to pray for them. With prophetic words, how I interpret a vision could be wrong, whereas there is less room for error when the person hears directly from God. I remember one time I was giving my friend a prophetic word and I told her that I saw that her father and he was bald. She corrected me by saying that her father was not bald, he had shaved his head. I haven't mentioned details about people's hair since then. Visions, I learned, can be open for interpretation and may become tainted through the lens of my own belief system.

I have learned there may be obstacles for people to receive visions or hear God's voice. Four common obstacles that I have observed are preconceived notions, background noise, striving, and having an agenda. Let me share a story that illustrates each obstacle.

One day a BSSM classmate asked me to pray for her and told me that she wanted to be closer to God. I asked her if I could pray for her to have an encounter and she said, "I already get encounters." She was taking a class that focused on encounters, but I knew it was a type of guided visualization. This type of encounter works for many people, but not for me. I get too hung up on hearing what the next step is going to be, which doesn't allow me to focus on what God is saying to me. I can't focus on two voices at once. I told my classmate that the type of encounter I was talking about is where God is the only one directing it, not another person. She still looked at me skeptically, so I asked her if the encounters she had in the class translated to a greater personal connection with God. Her answer was basically, "No, not really."

Eventually she allowed me to pray for her, and I asked her if she could imagine Jesus in front of her while I laid my hands on her head. She said, "No, I have never seen Jesus before." I couldn't believe her answer, because I knew that she was a painter and she could imagine images in order to paint them on canvas. I instructed her to just imagine someone who looked like Jesus. She then asked if I meant the image of Jesus that she saw in a certain painting. I said, "No. Jesus can appear differently to all of us. Just try to picture Jesus." She stood still for what seemed like an eternity while I was praying for her. When she finally opened her eyes about thirty minutes later, she said that God did talk to her.

Another time when I was on a mission trip, a woman was highlighted to me. When I asked her if I could pray for her, she said, "Maybe." On our day off I had a chance to pray for her. We started in a room where there were a lot of people coming and going, and she couldn't receive anything. I suggested we move to another room, but we had the same issue there. I thought that maybe if we could change the atmosphere, she could enter into an encounter, and the way that I had done that for myself in the past was to play a particular worship song, so I tried that. I used my phone to play my chosen song loudly on repeat to block all the other sounds. Thankfully, she then was able to have an encounter.

In a different situation, I approached a woman God highlighted to me, and she seemed a bit nervous. She began praying in tongues fervently as I was praying for her. I knew that she wasn't going to receive a vision from God if she was too focused on interceding for herself, so I told her to just receive. I do believe in interceding for yourself, but not when someone else is praying for you. I think this woman was interceding from a place of being fearful she would not receive everything that God had for her, and she was also striving to get God's blessings. She didn't understand what I said to her because she continued to pray in tongues, so I had to be direct and say, "This is a time for you to receive. You don't have to do anything else. Focus on the peace of God. Now ask Jesus what He wants to say to you." This enabled her to have an encounter.

My final example is a time when I prayed for a friend who was debating whether or not to apply for second year of BSSM (students can choose to attend the school for one, two, or three years). She was telling me about a dream that she had, which she thought was related to the decision she needed to make, and while she was talking about her dream, I heard God say that He wanted to talk to her. I prayed for her and told her that God might give her the answer that she was seeking. When I was finished praying I asked her if she received anything. She answered, "No." She said she saw Jesus and she was asking Him over and over again whether or not to apply for second year. Jesus didn't answer her at all.

It wasn't a complete surprise to me, because she didn't let God be God. She was trying to force her will onto God, and God is not a slot machine. God will answer when He wants to and not necessarily when we want Him to. God has certainly not answered every question that I have asked Him.

Another thing that my friend did not do was let the vision flow. She was trying to dictate the vision. If a vision moves or jumps to a difference scene, it's better to just go with the flow and ask Jesus questions along the way. When I prayed for my friend a second time, she told me that Jesus didn't talk to her about her decision, but He did talk to her about something that had even more bearing on her immediate future at the time.

After praying for numerous people to receive encounters, what I have learned is that God really wants to talk to every one of us. Almost one third of the prophetic words I've given have been relaying the message that God was asking people to spend more time with Him. Jesus is the same person today as He was in the Bible almost 2,000 years ago. God is a jealous God who wants our complete devotion to Him. It is His delight to speak to us and show us things personally. He doesn't want us to know about Him; He wants us to truly know Him. Encountering Him through visions is one of the best ways I have found for myself and for others to get to know Father God, Jesus, and the Holy Spirit intimately. Although there may be some mental barriers to overcome, once we get past them, sweet communion will be our reward.

SPIRITUAL ATTACKS
WHILE SEEING

I n the spirit realm there are positive as well as negative forces. The positive forces are God and His angels. The negative ones are the devil and his demons, which I refer to as "the enemy." It is important to realize that God is all powerful and the devil and his demons are not. God actually created the devil and demons as angels originally, but they rebelled against Him and became evil. Therefore they are not equal in power and authority to God and good angels. As Christians we also need to remember that Jesus defeated all the powers of darkness when He died on the cross and rose again, and He gave that same authority to us.

I often see demons as dark shadows in my visions, although I also see good angels as shadows. I know by the way I feel in the vision whether they are good or bad spirits. As I've mentioned, people (Christians and non-believers) can knowingly or unknowingly be influenced by angels and demons, which is often related to how they use their will to agree with God or the enemy. Evil spirits may also harass Christians sometimes, and I call these spiritual attacks.

Focusing on what the enemy is doing usually doesn't help the situation and can make me paranoid, but if I am being harassed, then I have learned that it is better if I deal with it head on. There are times when I am called to intercede for friends who are being attacked as well. Thankfully God has given me understanding and ways to deal with spiritual attacks. Let me start out by sharing a story that God used to teach me on why some believers are attacked.

I was interceding for my friend who was getting attacked repeatedly and I kept seeing dark shadows going after him. When I asked God to come into the vision, the shadows would go away, but then they would come back soon after. It became an endless cycle of dark shadows attacking my friend and then leaving and then attacking again. This was reflected in the turbulent time my friend was going through in real life. I was perplexed since my friend seemingly did nothing wrong to justify the repeated attacks on his life. He was a God-fearing man with very little sin in his life, and also a mighty warrior for God. I asked God time and time again to make the attacks stop because he didn't deserve them. God gave me a series of visions about my friend as an answer to my prayers.

In the first vision, I saw my friend with wings on his back that were being scorched from the bottom up to the top. I was horrified at the sight and did not want to see anymore, so I stopped watching it. Later that day, I decided that I wasn't going to let fear control me and I was going to call God into that vision. So, I revisited the vision by replaying it in my mind and again I saw my friend's wings getting scorched by little dark shadows. To stop from being scorched, my friend flew up toward Heaven to get away from the shadows. He was only safe for a little while until he got scorched again. He flew up higher to get away, but the same thing happened again and again until my friend was in Heaven where the shadows couldn't attack him. I saw him in Heaven saying, "Ha, ha, you can't get me now."

I felt the reason why my friend was getting continually attacked was because the shadows hated him. It wasn't exactly comforting for me to know that the shadows could keep attacking my friend until he went to Heaven. This is not to say that we can't bring Heaven to earth by ushering in God's presence and calling on God's protection. We do live in a fallen world where both good and evil will coexist until Jesus returns, but we must remember that God will always prevail. God knew I didn't feel good about this vision though, so He showed me another vision.

In the follow-up vision, I was talking to my friend and then I saw little dark shadows underneath my friend's wings attacking him and plotting new ways to attack him even more. Then I saw my friend in the throne room of Heaven facing God who was sitting on His white throne. Everything had a gold glow. God placed a huge crown and a long flowing robe on my friend. God said proudly, "He is mine."

My interpretation of this vision was that the demons were attacking my friend because they were jealous that he didn't belong to them. These attacks happened in attempt to get his focus off of God. I have always known my friend to be someone who praises God in all circumstances and who never says a harsh word against God. This showed me that believers can do all the right things and still be spiritually attacked. The phrase came to mind, "If the enemy is attacking you, then you must be doing something right."

The opposite can also be said. "If you're doing something wrong, the enemy can come and attack you." If you have any sin in your life, for example, it can create an open door for the enemy to walk in and attack you. This is not to say that all open doors stem from intentional sin. Open doors can be from generational curses, word curses against yourself, word curses against you from others, an unhealthy lifestyle, unforgiveness, judgmental attitudes, pride, jealousy, trauma, abuse, and fear. Please don't consider this a comprehensive list. Anytime there is an open door for any reason, you are allowing the enemy to have access to your life. Do whatever you can to shut any open doors to prevent this. I recommend asking God if there is an open door in your life, why it is open, and what you need to do to close it. Sometimes the key to closing the door is repenting for sin or forgiving someone else for sinning. Even if you don't have any open doors, as my friend did not, the enemy may try to get your focus off of God and onto him instead.

The key for my friend to escape the attacks in the vision was to go to Heaven. To me this meant he transcended his earthly circumstances to be fully immersed in an awareness of God and His presence. This can be done through worship or simply focusing our attention on God. From my personal experience, when I'm fully immersed in God's presence, I can only feel the peace of God and attacks don't affect me as much.

In my journey to seeing, there were many times the enemy attacked me to try to get me to stop going to church, stop praying, and to live in fear. Early on I had nightmares, which went away after a pastor prayed for me. But on the first night after I received the impartation for seeing, I had my first night terror. Night terrors are not the same as nightmares. They are realistic visions of being attacked by demons. In the night terrors I was having, I could feel and hear the thoughts of the dark shadows that were attacking me. I initially thought if I just ignored the night terrors, they would go away on their own. Sometimes ignoring attacks works because you're not giving the enemy the attention that he's seeking. Unfortunately, I continued to be terrorized for months until I was fearful of going to sleep. I tried praying before I went to sleep, asking people to pray for me, making positive declarations over myself, and reading the Bible before I went to sleep, but nothing worked. The only thing I could do to stop them was to force myself to wake up, but they would continue the next night.

One night, I was so fed up with having night terrors that instead of forcing myself to wake up, I decided to let the dark shadow come toward me and attack me. I wasn't going to let fear control me anymore. I challenged the dark shadow to do its worst, and I told it that I was ready to die. I thought that if it succeeded in killing me, at least I would be in Heaven with God. To my surprise, the dark shadow let out a deep sigh and it left. I haven't had perpetual night terrors since then, and when they do happen on occasion, I know how to stop them.

What I learned from this was to not let fear control me. The enemy was trying to make me afraid to see in the spirit realm and to render me unable to use the power and authority that God gave me. The truth is that the enemy can't really do anything to hurt me because I am a daughter of the King. I am thankful that God showed this to me once I finally stood up to face the enemy head on in the night.

He also showed me how to use my spiritual authority in my workplace. After I saw a vision of a dark shadow controlling my boss' mouth, I knew that demons were influencing my coworkers as well, so I grew very fearful. I had high anxiety as I wondered who would attack me next. I recognized that I always felt peaceful outside of work, so I started asking God for keys to maintaining that peace at work.

One day, while I was driving to work I was at the stop light right before my workplace, and all of the sudden I felt anxious. I knew that feeling was coming from a spirit lurking around my workplace. I got angry because I didn't want to have another stressful workday, so I started screaming in tongues for God to do something. He led me into a vision and I saw numerous dark shadows flying above my workplace, which made me upset. Then I saw an enormous image of Jesus smiling. He was standing over my workplace, looking straight at me with a rainbow over His head.

The dark shadows vanished as soon as Jesus showed up. After that, I no longer had any issues at my workplace and everything became peaceful again, like it was before the Halloween celebration. I felt God was teaching me about my authority, and letting me know that I can call on Him to fight any spiritual attacks that I face. God could have shown up at any time when I was praying for peace at my workplace, but He only showed up when I called on Him specifically to come into the situation, revealing my authority.

I used this same technique to pray for my friend who was getting spiritually attacked one day. My friend, who is a seer, could barely get out of bed. I couldn't visit him, so I prayed for him over the phone. We both saw little creatures with long nails attacking him, so I knew what to do next, which was to call on God to come into the situation. I started to travail over my friend, and then I saw random images for him that I didn't think pertained to what was going on with him at the time. I saw my friend as a frightened little boy in his childhood bedroom and I also saw him running from an approaching tornado into an underground shelter. After praying for a short time, I didn't see any more images, I only saw darkness, so I asked God to change that.

At first, I only saw a little light in one corner of my vision and as I continued to pray, the light kept getting bigger and bigger. When the light finally consumed the whole vision, it was only then I stopped praying for my friend and asked him how he was doing. He told me that the afflicting spirits left him, and that he was having a vision while I was praying for him. I don't remember what his vision was about, but he said that he did a prophetic act in the natural by opening and shutting his front door to let the spirits out of his house. What I learned from praying for my friend is that I could trust God to help even when I couldn't see Him in the spiritual realm.

Calling on God is not the only way to fight spiritual attacks. As I mentioned before, there is no cookie cutter way of doing anything with God. One time I couldn't stop a spiritual attack. I was having a disturbing vision of me harming myself that kept repeating in my head. I couldn't change the vision by calling God to come because of my emotional state of being, so I asked God what to do. God told me that I needed to be filled up with His presence in order for the tormenting vision to stop. He highlighted a man in the room who carried the presence well and who could fill me up. I went over to the man and asked him if he could lay hands on me, without telling him the reason why. When he laid his hands on me, immediately the tormenting vision stopped and I felt the peace of God again.

It is so important to be fully filled with God's presence. There won't be space for the enemy to influence us if we are saturated with God's love, hope, joy, and all the other good things that are part of His nature.

Not all attacks are the same, so it is best to ask God why the attack is happening and what to do about it. It's His delight to tell us the answer to these questions and it is not His heart for us to suffer. As we learn how to overcome spiritual warfare, we will gain confidence in who God is and who we are in Him.

THREE SIDES
OF GOD

A big benefit of the gift of seeing is the ability to discover different facets of God's personality. It's one thing to be told God is loving and joyful; it's another to experience and see it. I've had loads of encounters seeing Jesus that have shown me God's different personality traits. Three traits that have been repeatedly highlighted to me are His funny side, sassy side, and kind side. I am going to let these encounters speak for themselves, so I will simply share what I saw and not go into too much detail about what they meant to me. Enjoy the stories!

GOD'S FUNNY SIDE

In some of my encounters, God will poke fun at me to get me to lighten up since I tend to be too serious. Sometimes I have been annoyed with God's silliness, but one time God told me that I didn't truly love Him because I wasn't loving every part of Him, which includes His silly side. Since then, I've been trying to embrace my silly side.

CONFETTI HEAD

I was really missing Jesus one day, so when I saw Him in a vision I hugged Him tightly. While I was squeezing Jesus, His head turned into a balloon that started expanding until it popped with colorful confetti flying everywhere. I was stunned because Jesus, who had been in front of me, was no more. I walked around the corner and found Jesus snickering at me.

SCROLL TRUTHS

A lady was praying for me and told me to ask God what He thought about me. I went into a vision where I saw Jesus standing in front of me listing a lot of my great qualities. I wasn't receiving His words of affirmation at the time, so I rolled my eyes. Then He wrote everything He had said on a tan colored scroll with brown wooden handles. After He was finished writing, He rolled up the scroll and proceeded to hit me lightly on the head with it to get my attention with the truth of what He had said and to be funny at the same time.

DRAWING A CIRCLE

Jesus was drawing a circle with His finger in the air, and the circle became visible after He was done. I thought He was going to show me something profound within the circle, but He just popped the circle with His finger and it disappeared.

Then I went into another vision where I saw Jesus sitting on an inflatable yellow duck floating on a pool. He was wearing a Hawaiian shirt with black sunglasses and khaki shorts. He aimed His finger at me like a gun and said, "Gotcha."

CAT MASK

Jesus was wearing different clown masks to make me laugh, but I wasn't having any of it. I'm not into clowns in general. Then Jesus put on a cat mask with ribbons coming out of its ears. I let out a chuckle. He got me because He knew that I like cats and He also knew that I watched a cat video a couple of days earlier where a man scared his litter of kittens with a creepy cat mask.

GREENERY FOR DECORATING

I was asked to decorate the communion area in the Healing Rooms in a way that would usher in God's presence. The night before, I asked Jesus for a blueprint to help me know how to decorate well. In a vision I was in front of the communion area asking Jesus where I should place a certain picture. He just looked at me and then, to my absolute horror, He made the whole communion area explode into nothingness. This obviously didn't help me at all, so I got the hint that I could do whatever I wanted.

The next day while I was setting up the communion area,

I was thinking that I would like to have some greenery to decorate with. Unfortunately, it was too late for me to ask my leader to bring some from her house. The next thing I knew, my leader was walking in with a bag of greenery! She told me that she felt God nudge her to bring some from home, but she second guessed what she felt because she thought I had everything covered. As she was driving to the Healing Rooms, she realized she forgot her cell phone, and when she went back to get it she decided to bring the greenery with her too. The communion area that I was so worried about turned out looking great, and God did help me with the blueprint after all.

GOD'S SASSY SIDE

People who know me know that I'm a very sassy person. I can be sassy when I talk to Jesus, and Jesus is sassy back to me. Anything that I have thrown at Him, He has outwitted me with a comeback every single time, reminding me that He is much smarter than me. These are some of the most profound encounters I've had, which illustrate this side of Him.

PARTY POOPER

I was complaining to Jesus about my friend who jokes around too much when I went into a vision where I saw both of them having a party at a long wooden dining table. The table was decked out with party decorations, and it was too jovial for me. I used the white tablecloth that was covering the table to wrap all the decorations up into a huge ball. Jesus informed me that I missed a couple of decorations, so I gathered those up as well. The whole vision suddenly appeared black and white and dreary. I was sitting across from Jesus at the table and He told me that the world would be bland if we were serious all the time. He also told me that I didn't truly love Him because I didn't love all of Him; I only loved certain parts of him. I was shocked by His rebuke and agreed with Him, but I also told Him that I thought He went overboard with the vision. He laughed and said, "I got my point across, didn't I?"

GLOWING BALL

Jesus was gazing into a glowing ball, which peaked my curiosity. I went over to see what was so fascinating and I knew instantly that Jesus tricked me. There I was in the ball doing random deeds of kindness for other people! I didn't feel like what I had done was noteworthy, but Jesus was letting me know that He likes it when I do things for other people and that I'm interesting to watch.

GIVING JESUS GIFTS

I decided one day to give Jesus gifts to thank Him for all He has done for me. The first thing I gave Jesus was a piece of cake on a plate. He happily received it, but He gobbled it up and made a mess in front of me at the table. I was not amused. He knew that I don't like messes in general, and He only did that to be funny. I gave Him another piece of cake thinking that He would not do the same thing again to annoy me. He did the exact same thing! I made the decision to not give Jesus cake anymore after that.

The next day, I decided to give Jesus yellow flowers. Yellow is my favorite color and it reminds me of how happy Jesus is. I went into a vision where I became a little girl walking down a stone path. I yanked some yellow flowers up from the ground with the roots still attached. Jesus came toward me and stopped me just before I removed the roots to make the flowers more presentable to give Him. He told me that the roots were more important than the flowers because He cares more about the inside than the outward appearance. I was not expecting Jesus to give me a lesson through this gift.

Over a year later I decided to revisit the vision again. This time I was a young lady instead of a little girl, which signified my growth with God. I was mulling over all the possible gifts I could give Jesus who was standing next to me. I landed on a picture in a brown frame of Jesus and I sitting next to each other with our backs facing outward. Jesus looked pleased when I gave Him the picture. Then Jesus sat down looking at the picture in His hands with His back facing me. I felt His joy looking at the picture of us, but I felt what He really wanted was for me to sit next to Him and spend time with Him, just like we were doing in the picture.

TREE

I had a vision that I was in my yard trying to pull weeds unsuccessfully. After I pulled one weed out, a new one would pop up in its place. I couldn't understand why that was happening, but I was determined to pull all the weeds. I was working on one particular weed for a while, but it suddenly sprouted into a full-grown tree. I started to cry because there was no way to get rid of the weed now that it had become a tree. Then I saw Jesus pushing me on a swing that was hanging underneath the tree. People from all over started gathering around the tree and picking fruit from its branches. The tree not only benefited me, but it also benefited many people. Jesus told me that the tree represented a dream that He had given me, which I had been trying to dismiss.

GOD-GIVEN DREAMS

God gave me a dream for the future, which seemed impossible for me to ever accomplish in my lifetime. In my vision the dream was written on a piece of paper and I crushed it into a ball and then I flushed it down the toilet. I thought, "Good, I got rid of that dream," but then I felt someone behind me. It was Jesus. He pointed to a huge pile of wadded up balls of paper knowing that I couldn't possibly flush all those down the toilet, and then He winked at me. This powerfully illustrated that if God gives us a dream, there is nothing we can do to stop it from being fulfilled.

LOCKED UP HEART

One time in a vision I wrapped my heart securely with straps and a heart-shaped lock in the center so that no one could come in and hurt my heart anymore. I thought for sure that no one could break open my heart-shaped lock, but then I saw Jesus appear out of nowhere. He was smiling at me and said confidently that He had the key, which was in His hand. To my dismay, He easily opened my heart-shaped lock. I was upset that He opened me up so that I could get hurt again, but He filled my heart up with love. He hugged me and said He would protect me from all harm, and He told me that He was sorry for everyone who had hurt me in the past. After a moment He added that it wasn't right for anyone to hurt His precious child. I saw tears in His eyes when He said this to me.

GOD'S GIFTS

In this vision, both my friend and I were little children, but my friend was slightly older than me. We were both in front of Jesus who was giving each of us spiritual gifts. I felt that my friend, who I viewed as a mentor and a better steward, should get all my gifts, so I dumped my gifts onto his lap. At first my friend was confused, and then he didn't think what I did was right, so he dumped my gifts along with his gifts back onto my lap. We ended up going back and forth until Jesus stopped us by drawing a line on the floor and then separating us. He let us know that He's the one (and not us) who decides who gets certain gifts. Gifts are given through the grace of God and not because of our effort or good deeds.

HUGGING JESUS

I wanted to hug Jesus in a vision, but there was something preventing me. My arms were full of little containers that each held one of my worries. I knew I worried too much in general, which distracted me from focusing on God. In order for me to hug Jesus, I would have to let go of all my worries. Jesus showed me that I couldn't hug Him and my worries at the same time.

God's Kind Side

God is kind, but I often wonder if people really know how kind God truly is. I've been able to see how kind God is on a deeper level through my relationship and encounters with Him. I can't fully express how kind and loving God is, so allow my encounters to illustrate this side of His nature.

JESUS' TEARS

I was face to face with Jesus in a vision and His eyes started to well up with tears. He began crying and so did I. When I got upset that He was crying, His tears instantly vanished and He was smiling at me. He said, "Now you know how I feel when you cry." I had heard Jesus say audibly a couple of times, "Don't cry," when I was going through a period of sadness before I had this vision. This was Jesus' way of convincing me to not cry anymore.

PIT BULL FRIEND

When I was fasting from the internet and caffeine for four days, I received a vision where I felt the most loved by God thus far. I was a little girl walking on a long stone path and holding hands with Jesus. I was on the right side of Jesus, which to me represents a place of honor with God. Jesus was swinging my arm while we walked. I saw a giraffe and also a tiger along the pathway. Then I saw a brown pit bull dog walking beside me. Every time I looked at the pit bull's face, he was smiling at me.

We went to my parents' house and as soon as we were inside I wanted to leave because of painful memories, but Jesus was at the door to stop me. Then I saw both my parents become little children in front of me. God showed me how they had been hurt when they were young and vulnerable, which affected their behavior into adulthood. I felt empathy for them in that moment because I understood where they were coming from when they raised my twin brother and me. God helped me see my parents through a new lens, which made it easier to forgive them both, because it's hard to get mad at someone you see as a little child in pain.

The vision suddenly changed and I was in my childhood bedroom. Again, I wanted to leave because of painful memories, but Jesus stopped me. I became upset, but then I noticed that the pit bull was sitting next to me. He was smiling at me and comforting me with his presence. I realized that he had been with me the whole time, which I hadn't noticed. I was holding a small mirror in my right hand and I saw an image of myself as a sad little girl. I smashed the mirror into little pieces. Again, Jesus stopped me from leaving the room and He gave me a new mirror. In the new mirror I saw myself as a beautiful princess with a sparkly gown and a crown on my head. Jesus showed me who God made me to be, and how He sees me despite my past.

The pit bull was significant to me because it reminded me of four men who God brought into my life to guide me in my Christian walk. Just like I would be a bit nervous to meet a pit bull based on its appearance, I would not have talked to these four men if it hadn't been for God. However, I soon came to see that although they looked a bit rough on the outside, they had loyal and kind hearts. These men have truly blessed my life, and I'm thankful to God for them. God knew my heart's desire was to have a friendship with a father figure since my blood father was no longer in my life, and that is what the vision represented to me.

GOD'S GOT THIS

I was faced with a decision of whether or not to leave a ministry that I had been involved in for over a year. I had started serving somewhere else and I didn't have enough time to serve in both ministries, but I was having a hard time leaving the first ministry because I was worried about all the people that could be without help if I left. I was waiting for God to tell me what to do and He answered me with a vision. In the vision I saw Jesus smiling in front of me. He was leading me to join in the fun with some angels who were playing. Because I wasn't moving, He placed an arm around me to lead me toward them, but I felt conflicted since I kept seeing people that were suffering and needed help. I felt Jesus telling me it was okay and He had it covered, so I finally went with Him. In real life, I ended up leaving the first ministry. I needed to learn to trust that God meant it when He said, "I've got this."

PRAYING FOR A FATHER AND SON

One day in the Healing Rooms my prayer partner and I prayed for a father and his son who had autism. Nothing seemed to change in the son's condition when we prayed. It can be difficult emotionally when we pray for someone with a developmental disorder and we do not see immediate breakthrough, and I was feeling bad for the father and son after they left. My partner suggested that we pray for each other, and I went into a vision as soon as we held hands. I saw random images of the son and his father having a difficult life. After this, I felt a pressure on my right shoulder and then I saw tons of angels behind and beside me. Jesus was directing all the angels to go out the door to find the father and son and to take care of them. When the angels left and I was all alone with Jesus, He comforted me by hugging me, and I felt His love completely consume me.

I AM NOT ALONE

In a vision I was standing in the middle of nowhere, and then I saw someone coming toward my right side. I realized it was the Holy Spirit, and then I saw Jesus on my left side and Father God in front of me. The three of them formed a circle around me, and I was in the center of it. God took my spirit out of my body and I floated up until I was looking down at my body. Angels, too numerous to count, surrounded the circle. God was showing me that I am truly never alone in this world.

A NEW CREATION

I became Christian at the age of 35, so I had plenty of time before then to live a sinful life. I was having a hard time believing that God sincerely forgave all my past sins, and I asked God almost daily if He had forgiven me. God finally answered me with a vision while I was attending a conference out of town. I felt tingling on my head and I instantly saw myself wearing a gold crown that was burning with flames. Soon the fire consumed all of me, and I became a pile of ashes with the burned crown resting on top of the pile in a dark cave. Jesus appeared at the cave's opening and started blowing the ashes away. When the ashes were completely gone, I emerged as a glowing newborn baby, symbolizing that I had become a new creation in Christ. Then Jesus carried me out of the cave toward a group of people who were His family. The vision ended with me being accepted by this new family and feeling a heavy burden being lifted off of me. After I had this vision, I no longer thought about my past sins because I had confidence knowing that God forgave me.

GOD'S ADVICE REGARDING STOCK OPTIONS

The first time I believed I heard God's voice was when I was 29 years old and I wasn't Christian. My boss, who was also the owner of the company I worked for, asked me privately what I wanted to do with my stock options. He advised me to wait to sell my options and receive more money as they increased in value down the road. I heard a quiet voice in my head telling me to sell everything. I blurted out, "I want to sell all of my options," without thinking. Immediately, I wanted to take back what I said as I saw a hurt look on my boss' face. He thought that I didn't believe in the profitability of his company. My decision to sell wasn't what everyone else was doing or what my boss wanted me to do, so I wasn't even sure why I trusted the voice.

The stock options tanked a year later and were worth less than a dollar. The money I received from selling the options was the amount I needed for the down payment of my house ten years later. I had saved the money for all those years, just waiting for the right time to spend it. I knew it was a gift from God. This story shows that God has always taken care of me, even before I was a believer.

INNER VOW

My housemate's friend came to visit her at my house and we started chatting. She asked me what my first childhood memory was, and I told her it wasn't good. She responded by asking me if I could replay the childhood memory in my head and then ask God where He was during that time. To my surprise, I went into a vision where I was a 3-year-old girl, and I was looking through a crack on the hinge side of a door, watching my twin brother go to the bathroom. I was pointing with one finger through the door crack at my brother's private part innocently, because I didn't have one. My brother saw me looking at him, so he closed the door, which inadvertently crushed my finger. I started wailing and Jesus stepped in and gently removed my hurt finger from the door. I didn't feel the pain after that.

Jesus told me that I had made an inner vow to protect myself at that moment. I associated my brother's private part as being bad because I felt pain when my finger was crushed, so to protect myself from further hurt, I believed the lie that all male's private parts are bad. This was the root cause of my bisexuality, which I suffered with for over 15 years.

I never once acted on my urges toward anyone of the same sex because I knew those urges were morally wrong, but I couldn't have any close female friends and I had issues with male partners. I had received prayer on a number of occasions, but it didn't change my feelings. It was something that I learned how to deal with, but God changed that one day when He told me that He made me straight. When I had the vision of my 3-year-old self, I knew what God had told me was true. I no longer struggled with bisexual feelings anymore. After that I was able to make some female friends too.

When Jesus stepped into my vision, He released me from my inner vow to protect myself from men that I wasn't even aware had been plaguing me. It was only through God's grace and God's kindness that I was completely healed of bisexuality. God continues to work on my other issues as well because He wants me to be fully healed and whole.

FORCED TO GET PRAYERS

I was in a church service listening to a guest speaker's testimony about how he reconciled with his father, and I was emotional because my relationship with my father was still broken. I don't like getting emotional in front of people, so I was hoping no one saw my tears. The leaders said they were planning on giving healing words of knowledge at the end of service. I had a feeling that I would get called out for prayer, because I knew that it is God's nature to comfort me when I'm upset. I told God several times, "Please don't let me get called out for prayer. I don't want anyone to pray for me right now. I'd rather be in pain than get prayer." It may sound silly, but I was adamant about not receiving prayer.

When they started giving words of knowledge for healing, someone said she felt the urge to pray for someone in the room who became a Christian on October 16th. I was thinking, "Oh crap. That word is so specific." I looked around to see if anyone was responding, but no one else stood up. Although I wanted to stay seated, I didn't want the person who gave the word to feel like they missed it, so I stood and ended up receiving prayer. This encounter showcased God's funny, sassy, and kind personality traits. God was funny since He got the last laugh, God outsmarted me by knowing what would make me stand up, and God was kind since He ultimately wanted me to receive prayer.

Epilogue

I f you haven't been able to see into the spiritual realm, I release a blessing to you based on John 16:24, that you will ask and you will receive. As you have read, God has given me many of my heart's desires. I pray that God does the same for you.

God is personal and speaks to each of us in a language we can understand. God talks to me mostly through visual stories because that is how I'm able to retain information. When I was young and in school, if I had to memorize anything I would make up little stories so I could see how everything connected and remember it. If God talked to me using Scripture references, I would forget almost instantly unless I would write them down. The point I'm trying to make is that God wants a relationship with you, and it is His delight to talk to you in a way that you will best understand.

Thank you for going on this journey with me. May your relationship with God deepen, may your joy and peace increase, and may you never lose sight of what matters.